Praise for **NAOMI REPLA**

"Naomi Replansky must be counted among the most brilliant American poets. That she has not received adequate praise is one of the major mysteries of the world of poetry." —GEORGE OPPEN

"Naomi Replansky's poetry rings with reality and wisdom, and it is always song. Her observant, political wit and gravity are as piercing and as necessary now as ever—and I would say more so ... her voice and her way of reading are among the very best we have." —JEAN VALENTINE

"It is no exaggeration to state that she shares in power of truth, in precision of phrasing with the best of Sylvia Plath. She is master of her style in the heat and sorrow of her poems. She is in control, but the poems take off." —DAVID IGNATOW

"The free and savvy poems of Naomi Replansky soar, in a speech that urgently affirms a strength we've almost forgotten we have. Clear as water and as necessary, they quicken our solitary selves. The light pulse of their instantly shared energy shows us each other and joins us in our eagerness to speak out as they do, against confusion. They are bold and embolden us ... To participate in power is freedom, Cicero says. These poems, proposing sixty years of a free woman's song, wake us up to it. Their cadences and claims uncover the given world and make us think. We do so willingly because the beat they keep is the rhythm of the heart." —MARIE PONSOT

"Along with Auden, Cavafy, and Crane, Naomi Replansky has been one of the important models in my writing. Her work taught me essential things and embodies the essence of what poetry is about." —EDWARD FIELD

"If a voice like Naomi Replansky's can't be seen as central to our nation's 'wealth' of poetry, then maybe canonization itself needs to be radically re-conceived. In any case, Replansky's poems are finally available to a generation of readers who have been looking for them without knowing it...." —ERIC GUDAS

Also by **NAOMI REPLANSKY**

Ring Song (1952)
Twenty-One Poems, Old and New (1988)
The Dangerous World: New and Selected Poems, 1934–1994 (1994)

COLLECTED POEMS

NAOMI REPLANSKY

COLLECTED POEMS

Black Sparrow Press | Boston | 2023

First Published in 2012 by BLACK SPARROW PRESS

GODINE
Boston, Massachusetts
www.godine.com

LIBRARY OF CONGRESS CATALOGING-IN-PUBLICATION DATA
Replansky, Naomi.
[Poems]
Collected poems / by Naomi Replansky.
p. cm.
ISBN 978-1-57423-215-8 (alk. paper)
I. Title.
PS3568.E676A16 2012
811'.54—dc22
2010049279

Fifth Printing, 2023
Printed in the United States

Once again,
to
Eva Kollisch
... Old-age bonus granted me
Against all probability...

and
to the memory of my parents,
Fannie Replansky
and
Sol Replansky

CONTENTS

PART II: POEMS FROM *THE DANGEROUS WORLD* (1994)

PART III: NEW AND UNCOLLECTED POEMS

PART I

POEMS FROM *RING SONG* (1952)

FOREWORD

Traveler, this is no fountain.
Wounded, I am no healer.
Hungry, not one word here
is as good as bread.

Not only for that
do I ask forgiveness.

Forgive me my unwritten poems:
how many have I trampled,
how many ignored.

Lazy or blind or
fearful I ignored them.
Yet they swarmed everywhere,
the unwritten poems.

Forgive me the colors
they could have worn.

Forgive me the faces
that do not look out
from these lines.

This book is too small.
Under each heavy
hour of my silence
died a poem, unheeded.

1950

TALISMANS

A moss-decked proverb
In the sea-lapped sand.
A man-sized doubt
In a god-fearing land.

A flap-shoed walker
In a gold-paved town.
A blue-black wound
In a white-faced clown.

A two-sided riddle
In a one-way path.
A dove-wing folded
Over red-eyed wrath.

A stone-dry gaze
From the tear-sogged slime.
A spider-kiss scuttling
Through a close-mouthed rhyme.

1940s

THE INVISIBLE MAN

I often see the invisible man,
That wandering man, and see him easily.

And still I know it is not I he seeks.
I am too close, I am like family.
Because I need no argument to see him,
Even my arms around him cannot prove him
More than a dream of dreaming, more than cloud.

Ah, but the others, the solid citizens!
To them he lifts a face that could be flesh,
Be features, and be lovely, be a face.
And they walk towards him and he smiles in pride.
And they walk through him and he droops in shame.
"You can't do that!" he cries, "I am no highway!
"If only I had clothing you would see me!
And must I shoot a gun for you to hear me?"
But they walk through him and their path lies open
And their five senses not for him are sharp.

He turns again to me. I can do nothing.
Still, if you could see us, us two locked
In our occasional fantastic embrace,
See, it is friendly, because profitless,
But always restless, and away we lean,
The head turned sideways and the glance averted,
Seeking the others solider than us

Whose five senses always served them well
But whose five senses not for us are sharp.

1947

[17]

THE HUNTERS

They went hunting lions
But a flea attacked them
And their hunters' passion
Narrowed to a flea.

Can they tell their story
When the other hunters
Stand around like fountains
Headless in the dawn?

In the bloody morning
They will tell their story.
They have still their tongues, who
Never lost their heads.

1942

EPITAPH: 1945

My spoon was lifted when the bomb came down
That left no face, no hand, no spoon to hold.
A hundred thousand died in my home town.
This came to pass before my soup was cold.

THE SIX MILLION

They entered the fiery furnace
And never one came forth.
How can that be, my brothers?
But it is true, my sisters.
They entered the fiery furnace
And never one came forth.

No god came down, my brothers,
To breathe on them, my sisters.
Their bodies made a mountain
That never touched the heavens.
Whose lightning struck the killers?
Whose rain drowned out the fires?
My brothers and my sisters,
No angel leaned upon them.
No miracle could shield them
From the cold human hands.

1946

COMPLAINT OF THE
IGNORANT WIZARD

Whoever gave me magic told me lies.
This laying on of hands works otherwise.

Every whirling part of me is warm
Yet I come down on here like a snowstorm.

I speak the word that might unlock the rock
But hard upon that word my two jaws lock.

My sleeping power gathering to leap
Leaps tooth and claw into a deeper sleep.

The love potion I slyly pour for one
Is by another seized and swallowed down.

I learned the speech of birds; now every tree
Screams out to me a baleful prophecy.

Into a statue's lungs I breathe my own.
Sighing, it fills me with this sigh of stone.

My answer to the riddle bears with it
A greater riddle and more desperate.

All, all runs wild, all wild and uncontrolled.
A toad hops from my mouth instead of gold.

1949

THE BALLOON

I cut my cords, I scrapped my weight,
I rose up free and separate,
And since no move was made to hold me down,
I said, "Why, I am quits then with this town
Where nothing holds me down."

And so I rise.
But the ascent is slow.
Street, window, and roof,
It is no easy thing to shake you off.
O city, how I hold you with my eyes.
They were so long seduced, will not let go.
They still are passionate
And still insatiate.
A bloody business this, to tear away my eyes,
But it is done.

And I float free
Into an air so rare
That nothing holds me in.
An air so thin, no pressure now at all.
The charge of life in me
That down below seemed light, lighter than air,
Now clamors heavily,
All ways and outwards, battering the thin
Wall of my skin.
I burst, I fall.

Paris, 1950

HOUSING SHORTAGE

I tried to live small.
I took a narrow bed.
I held my elbows to my sides.
I tried to step carefully
And to think softly
And to breathe shallowly
In my portion of air
And to disturb no one.

But see how I spread out and I cannot help it.
I take to myself more and more, and I take nothing
That I do not need, but my needs grow like weeds,
All over and invading; I clutter this place
With all the apparatus of living.
You stumble over it daily.

And then my lungs take their fill.
And then you gasp for air.

Excuse me for living,
But, since I am living,
Given inches, I take yards,
Taking yards, dream of miles
And a landscape, unbounded
And vast in abandon.
And you dreaming the same.

1946

RING SONG

...When that joy is gone for good
I move the arms beneath the blood.

When my blood is running wild
I sew the clothing of a child.

When that child is never born
I lean my breast against a thorn.

When the thorn brings no reprieve
I rise and live, I rise and live.

When I live from hand to hand
Nude in the marketplace I stand.

When I stand and am not sold
I build a fire against the cold.

When the cold does not destroy
I leap from ambush on my joy...

1944

NOSTALGIC MEMORY OF NEW YORK

When you come back to,
Come back to the city,
Do not stand and wonder
 —Will it take me back?

It will take you back.

When you look down the
Streets you deserted
They will not rise up
To shake you off,

You, the unfaithful.

The wild automobiles
Will not rear in anger
Nor the gears clash
And their teeth be broken

Just to behold you.

The buildings that never
Bowed down in grief
To see you depart
Will take you back

With their heads high.

And the rush-hour crowd
Will sweep you off your feet
And the short-order cook
Will sizzle you in fat.

Be proud of your welcome.

1946

THE JOURNEY HERE

One night when it was midnight in the bed
I turned my head and said:

This red thread of error looped around my wrist
Leads far away.
I cannot now untwist
Myself antagonist
From childhood stampings, from streets fierce in play.

I stumbled through the thicket of the law,
I wrestled, losing, with a man of straw,
I reared at shadows and I walked on cloud.
And from the fugitive I took
The many-colored cloak
And wore it somberly, as though a shroud.
I loved when sure of loss
Then stood and cursed my loss
And swore myself star-crossed.
And though I found a word, though at my breast
I warmed a word, I still was like the bird
That broods the offspring of another's nest.

I was, I did, but I will let it be.
Tonight I must hold dear
Whatever brought me here.
These days of mine that ran in anarchy
From this rare midnight seem
Single with purpose, seem
The slow unfolding of a single theme
That led
Most gently to this midnight and this bed.

1945

THE SIGHTSEERS

On a Saturday night the blessèd
Come to the dance-hall of the damned.
It is so good to feel so blessèd,
It is so good not to be damned,

That they must smile at one another,
And then they sometimes dance together,
And watch the damned who dance together
And dance so close with one another.

Their faces show how they are damned.
Yet when they dance, they dance exalted.
The blessèd swear—Well we'll be damned!
How can they dance as if exalted?

This is a steaming underworld:
Where are the writhings? Where the cries?
We came down from our overworld
To see them writhe, to hear their cries.

But would they make of this a church
And hand on waist bless one another?
The blessèd look at one another:
—We did not come to be in church.

The blessèd shudder in this air,
The steaming air around the damned,
And flee into the outside air
That tells the blessèd from the damned.
Cool as a judge, the outside air
That tells the damned just how they're damned.

1951

THE VISITOR

This day a simple day
that comes for a visit
that comes to sit quiet.

Yet I in such small grace
receive my visitor.
I watch it narrowly
and wonder, Friend or foe?
I ransack it for weapons
then question it with passion:
What message? What message?

But this is a mute and unassuming day.

And is a good guest
and brings small gifts.
I must learn again to give it welcome.

1945

SIDESHOW

A little show to tease
A little show to please
To enlighten
And to frighten

THE HALF-MAN HALF-WOMAN

How can he-she ever rest
When the beard denies the breast?
She would wake when he would sleep
She would swoon when he would leap
She must shun what he pursues
Down divided avenues.

You who come and ask for love,
Who below and who above?
Turn about
In doubling doubt.
Not you nor two wild horses can
Tear this woman from this man.
They are locked forever in
This battleground, this single skin.

THE MAMMOTH MAN

They stand around to hear him laugh
And he will laugh
And when he laughs, how much will laugh!
That whole form
Big as a whale and mammal-warm.
And the onlookers swarm around
To warm themselves upon that sound.

But should he stare
From wintry acres of despair,
Then slim and trim
Will flee from him
Will flee that cold and never know
If any warmth still lives below
His every crevice filled with snow.

THE QUICK-CHANGE ARTIST

Rubber-jointed, loose of limb,
He is what you think of him,
For he takes his shape and size
From the image in your eyes.

Nine these lives and none his own:
Is a stone and can be thrown,
Is a reed and can be bent,
Is a coin and can be spent.

He can curl within a hand
Or be spanned across a land,
Can be victor or be lost,
Can be solid or be ghost.

When you turn away your eyes,
Then what size? And what disguise?
In that dark he must retrace
The features of his single face,

Find alone his lone desire
And his solitary fire
And his separate flesh and bone
And his unique martyrdom.

THE TATTOOED LADY

Step up and see
the lady's past
set down in ink
from head to heel.

The names, the flags,
the arrowed hearts,
a face within
a flaming wheel.

The dragon of terror
curls at her nipple
and song-birds settle
upon her thighs.

Ah she is public,
the tattooed lady,
smooth to the touch,
a feast for the eyes.

Leaf through her skin,
who runs may read.
All is set down,
it is not to erase.

What now to be written,
be sketched, be stippled?
Is there one blank space
in a secret place?

1941

THE CONSTANT SUICIDE

Heavily, heavily
You leap into the painted sea
And dry and bruised return to us
Breathing heavily.

"I will twine me of my life
I will not use a wooden knife
There is no trapdoor to my grief
And in my cries no trickery!"

Angrily, angrily
You dash through cardboard scenery
And in the painted desert lie
Dying angrily.

1943

WHODUNIT?

All through the valley of Whodunit
Falls the shadow of Why.
Loud is the sob of the one who runs,
Loud is the hunters' cry.

For crime was done and one faced one
And a gun spoke one-two-three
And snow running down from the mountaintops
Was blood when it reached the sea.

Who could have done this dreadful deed
If it wasn't me or you?
O cover the valley for a track
And comb it for a clue.

It wasn't me it wasn't you
It was the man they chase.
He's cornered there in a cowering fear
The blood flies away from his face.

The audience leans back to breathe
The hunters take a bow
The headlines clap their bold applause:
Whodunit's done for now!

The hunters hang onto their man
And merrily pass by
Where I scot-free and you scot-free
Stand in the shadow of Why.

1936

IN THE SNOW MOUNTAIN

In the snow mountain I cannot build a snow-man.
I grow a bone-dry cactus.
From the desert I beseech all drowned ones:
—One drop of water!

Born of a war, I was always aching and straining
To nuzzle myself into peace.
Peace when it came was hunted and haunted, and stayed
Just for a moment.

In silence is the smell of treachery, and sanction
Of hunger, and therefore I shout.
But in the storm of sound I clothe myself
In a hush like fur.

Here who sins the birthday sin of the wrong
Skin or god, finds that the sin is mortal.
Tense with that idiot guilt, how could my gestures
Ever come easy?

How is it with me, that I assail these lips
With craft, and art, and no real wish to win?
Leave the warm arms for the windy streets
And breathe more freely?

I run towards the gleaming eyes of ports and children
But they are whole, and go their own sweet way.
Who winced at doorbells, pauses sick with envy
At lighted windows.

Unmade by what has made me, I see
In blinding colors the visions of the blind,
I too being driven by such savage desire
And saved thereby.

1936

[34]

THE END

How long say how long
Can a lone animal
Devour its young
And its race not vanish.

So long just so long
Can these colors and sounds
Wander and be rich
In the sealed tunnel.

1943

THOUGH FAILURE HUGGED YOU
LIKE HEAT

Though failure hugged you like heat
and glistened like sweat
it has its winds and its change
like any atmosphere.

And though you wandered wide
and came back empty-handed
you will have as many loves
as you have doors opening on the world.

And there are many mornings
arriving so thickly veiled:
a knife between the teeth?
a rose between the teeth?

1942

YOU WALKED A CROOKED MILE

You walked a crooked mile
you smiled a crooked smile
you dropped a wandering tear
all in a crooked year.

When there was one kiss
against ten curses
and one loaf
against ten hungry
and one hello
against ten goodbyes
the odds stalked
your crooked steps.

And you turned no corner
without heart-tightening
and against ten cannon
you had one fist
and against ten winters
you had one fire.

1938

EVEN THE WALLS HAVE EARS

Even the walls have ears.
I'd better swallow my soul
as damning evidence,
swallow my soul,
swallow it whole.

You'd better swallow your soul.
Its very scars are treason.
Your soul is contraband
they will destroy
easier than understand.

We'd better scrap our skins,
a damning damning clue—
a drainpipe will do!
If they should find our skins
we're done for, me and you.

We're done for anyway.
The trial is quick and once,
and our involved defense
takes our whole lives to say.

We're damned by evidence:
behold our skins, our souls.

1944

RESTLESS DIALOGUE

What do you see, honey,
Tell me what you see.
I see this passion dwindled to a pinpoint,
Pinpoint, swordpoint, a knife for stabbing.

What do you hear, honey,
Tell me what you hear.
I hear a crowd mobbing a delicate secret,
The race-law shouted and the lynch-cross hammered.

But I am here, honey,
Feel me, I am here.
Yes, you are here, with your volcano tenderness,
Running tongue of lava to enfold but not harm me.

Close as can be, honey,
Our bodies are close.
But also are drumskins stretched many miles around us.
Heels beat upon us a tattoo of anger.

They cannot find us, honey,
Not if we are quiet.
Maybe not find us, maybe be quiet,
Maybe be strangled in straitjacket quiet.

What do you want, honey,
Tell me what you want.
Anything but lie here, anything but listen.
Swordpoint, knife-edge, at last turn outward.

1945

[39]

A VISIT TO THE ZOO

See the poet.
Will it bite?
Sometimes, if aroused.

Feeds? On anything.
A word ate a tear,
ate a laugh, ate love,
swallowed anger, gulped down hope.
A word ate a word made of venom, of honey,
and still came back hungry.

So that, when they see the poet,
some people are always slightly ashamed,
and withdraw warily,
because hunger has such a big mouth,
opening everywhere, even in crowds.

But when poem comes forth free,
many take it in,
and not even from pity.
—*O smallfire! My hands are cold!*
Trumpet! Prickling of desire!
Thundering landscape! That speech is mine!
I lived that face, I wept those tears!
Then my life played will also be music!

The listeners, laughing and weeping,
cover the poem with kisses.

And the poet, what of the poet?
It is in the cage.
Its poems spring from it

as the black curls did from Samson:
haven of secrets,
hoarding of strength,
shorn of them it shivers.

1937

JUMP RHYTHM

Well that jump rhythm
say that jump rhythm
it took me by the waist
when I was feeling bad.

Sweat stood upon me
and said - This is better!
Whiskey exploded
in splinters of breathing.
And horn drum and piano,
the horn drum and piano!

And everybody whispered
soft and loud like bloodbeats
— Now are you hot and bothered?
but sister so are we
sister so are we.

I did not wish to hear them
but faster than remembering
they took me by the waist
when I was feeling bad.

Until I felt the bad mood gone
and openhearted looked down upon

the floor gathering like a wound.

1941

IN SYRUP, IN SYRUP

In syrup, in syrup,
In syrup we drown,

Who sell ourselves
With a sparkling smile.

Padded with pathos
Our winding sheet.

The bomb bounded
By buxom beauties.

Horror gelded
By the happy ending.

How can we swim
Who hold to our haloes?

Down we go, down
In syrup, in syrup.

1946

THE MONEY-TREE

— When you are tall, you who are small,
Then take this word from me:
It's only your brow's honest sweat
Will grow the money-tree.

— Now I am tall my sweat falls down,
And honest all the time,
But scant and silver is the yield,
And thin as the thinnest dime.

— Look here, goodlooking, life is short,
Grab from it what you can.
It's arms apart, and wide the heart,
And catch a wealthy man.

— It's arms apart, and wide the heart,
And who comes marching in
But some poor guy with a loving eye
To make my hunger twin.

— All's double-cross, and yours the loss,
So why not share the loot?
O fling your coins in the field of chance
And watch the tree take root.

— The cards are marked, the dice are fixed,
My horses all run lame.
By skill or luck, by hook or crook,
I cannot beat the game.

Now when she died she died in pain,
In honest sweat died she.
Then with the special eyes of death
She saw the money-tree.

Its roots were knotted in her hands,
Sprang from her hair and hide.
It was from herself, herself,
The tree grew fair and wide,
While strangers plucked the last green buds
Before she wholly died.

1940

TAKE THE SNAKE

Take the snake that lies coiled
In the drunkard's bed.
No knife can sap the poison sac
In that glittering head.

Take the planes that zoom back
To the bomb-shocked eyes.
Where is the ack-ack or flak
Will ever clear those skies?

Skin once ribboned by a whip
Scars to anything:
A feather-touch, a wind, a word,
Sets it shuddering.

In the lap of lack what seed
Fills and will not spill?
Quick to fist its nightmare fight
Famine crouches still.

1947

TWO WOMEN

There is a woman climbing a glass hill
Of clothes and dishes on a dusty floor;
Today surmounted, tomorrow towers still.

There is a woman opening like a door.
Many come in, but only she is bitch.
Empty, is filled, then empty as before.

There are two women, standing, and on each
Is smiled salvation or is howled damnation,
And, saved or damned, must still stay within reach.

Until the end,
When all are served, the sermons and the omens,
The preachers served, the children and the elders,
And still they come,
And still demand,
And still stand on her floor and ask for more.

And still the clipped wing leans against
Her eagle of experience.

1938

FOREIGNER

He is alone and unarmed
And has no vessel for his vanity.
His curse is spoken, but nothing trembles.
His praise like rain runs down the gutters.

Laughter seizes him and he is silent.
Grief shakes him, he hides it in a stare.
And he can change nothing where he passes
Though he walk barefoot through bristling events.

A room, a sea, a street, a war,
Gather within and sinew him for speech
Richer than this, but who will hear him out.
O who will know him unto nakedness.

1950

CEREMONY

Who put the mask of Whiteskin on?
"I," said the freckled,
"I," said the mottled,
"I," said the pinkcheeked,
"I," said the grayface,
"We put up our hands and we stopped the sun
And we put the mask of Whiteskin on."

Here one comes knocking without the mask:
"Closed," says the textbook,
"Packed," says the jury,
"Don't drink me," the water,
"Don't pass me," the front door,
"Only white dung,"
Cries the sacred outhouse,
"Is a pale hand upon me?"
Asks the mystic machine,
"Boy!" calls a tongue
To dwindle a black man,
"It is death to enter and death to ask
If you come knocking without the mask."

Who dances this magic of race and face?
"I," said the hungry,
"Though hunger is skinless."
"I," said the fearful,
"Though fear has no face."
"I," said the safe one,
The loomlord, the landlord,
"Gave hunger a skin,
Gave fear a face.
Now take your place and remember your place
And dance to this magic of race and face."

1939

THE RATLESS CAT

When I came home my mother cat said,
"Tom," she said, "I wish I was dead."
When I came home my father cat bawled,
"It's cats like you make it tough for us all!"
When I came home my brother cat scratched me
And said he wished a dog would catch me.
When I came home my sister cat said,
"You put the gray hairs in mama cat's head."
When I came home my grandpa cat spat,
"You ruined the last years of a feeble old cat!"

When I came home without a rat,
Mom, pop, brother, sis, and grandpa cat
Took one long look, gave one loud groan,
When I came home, when I came home.

1934

EPITAPH: HERE I BE

HERE I BE
I LIVED TO SEE
MY PROPHETS HONORED IN THEIR OWN COUNTREE
MY HEROES HALOED EVEN BACK AT HOME
THEN KNEW I SURELY MY OLD AGE WAS COME
AND CALLED IT QUITS AND CREPT INTO MY TOMB

1946

A BRICK NOT USED IN BUILDING ...

A brick not used in building
Can smash a window pane.
For anyone with ears to hear
Let it be said again.
A brick not used in building
Can smash a window pane.

1943

A GOOD DAY'S WORK

Whose dog am I?
The time-clock's dog.
Whose dog are you?

Learn how to smile at foremen.
A dirty joke and time for a smoke.
Be slick, be quick, be human.

The night is small
And hard to hold,
Sinks into the spongy morning.
The day is large
And hard to pass
And I can't go over it
And can't go under it
And can't go around it
But must go through it

And me dogtired.

1944

THE SONG THAT WENT ON
DURING THE TRAGEDY

"Let them not bother me,"
 said the tree by the river.
"Why do they bother me
 with their howling by the river?"

"Let her not carry me,"
 said the child deep inside.
"Why does she carry me
 with that sorrow deep inside?"

"Let him not utter me,"
 said the word in the throat.
"Why does he utter me
 as though I blistered his throat?"

> But he in his shouting,
> and she in her fury,
> they never heard,
> how could they hear
>
> the word in the throat,
> the child deep inside,
> the tree by the river?

1941

ONCE THERE WAS A MAN

Once there was a man
who turned one day into silence.
Not anger, which has its shouting,
not betrayal, which at last confesses,
not murder, which they say will speak.
He turned into a silence
whose sucking hollow
strips my face from me like a glove.

If he never calls, as he will not,
what shall I tell my breasts?
"Pull in your beaks, my pigeons.
The stranger who gave you food
and you thought it would be forever
has gone from this park for good."

If he never calls, as he will not,
how dare I tell our story?
My words may turn into stones
as easily as a man
turned one day into silence.

1944

DISMISSAL

O you pointless grief,
Go, fall headfirst
Into the soft stickiness of absurdity.

O you worthless love,
Go, practice a snarl.

For how can I justify you?
You are neither warriors nor wisdom.
You are the sand in the machines.
In the speed you are the slowness.

Because truth jostled excuse
In my red-raw throat
I could not even make of you
A myth that would be a mountain.

You inhabit me wastefully.
Therefore I banish you.
Get you gone, both of you.
I shall soon follow.

1947

I KNOCKED UPON
YOUR WINDOWPANE

—I knocked upon your windowpane,
I pounded at your door,
I slammed and whammed my wish for you
Until my hands were sore.

—A craziness lives with me here,
A fever holds me close,
Else none so quick as I would be
To let you in my house.

Now jealous were you, hearing this,
You standing locked outside?
No words from you however loud
Can open that door wide.

You have no need to twist his wrist
Or knock on his headache
Or seven times to shout his name
To make sure he's awake.

But follow hard, through flame and flood,
Where obscure signposts lead
Until you come at last to touch
His vibrant nerve of need.

And follow hard, through stun and shock,
And finally observe
Its branches clutched at anything
To ground the live-wire nerve.

—Come out, come out, although outside
The frost bites to the bone.
Who then so free as you to be
Actor, though acted upon.

—A craziness lives with me here,
Its face with fever glowing.
It holds me close, it holds me dear,
This demon lover with me here
Who woos with wool the shorn lamb where
Untempered winds are blowing.

1938

WHEN I MELT DOWN

When I melt down in your furnace
I want to take shape in your mold.
Blast me, cast me, change me,
Before the wind turns cold.

Look, from the red-hot center
I lift up my white-hot face.
My nose finds its bridge as always,
My eyes flow back into place.

Neither destroyed nor diamond
I walk from the core of your flame,
The rain does not hiss when it hits me,
And I answer to my old name.

1944

BLIND MAN

Blind man on the train
Caresses his girl's knee,
As if in privacy.

I, seated opposite,
Glance at them all the way.
At close of long day
Upon my blankened mind
Scene fastens, to find
Ready response to it.

I, being city-bred,
Never was quite alone,
Never was islanded,
Always must turn my head
To watch the passerby
With over-careful eye,
Moody with change outside,
Quicksilver's proper bride,
Servant to circumstance,
And like a mirror to
The funeral or dance.
Easy besieged am I,
All my defenses down:
What this or that one said
Made me queen or clown.

Now not for simplicity
Nor crowd-begot privacy
Would I trade my sight.
But still, blind man,

On you my eyes alight,
My eyes, chameleon-vexed,
Darken upon your night:

I take you as my text.

1937

FIRST LOVE

Yes, there was this, and I remember all:
I remember, yes, there was, deep in the bed,
Loud at the window, taut against the wall,
The scolding city of my maidenhead.

I lay, held a mirror, slept,
Listened to night sounds,
Played with nouns,
While a mouse crept
And a child wept.

Then who sprang but you,
Wherever I looked,
The work to undo.
To set me on your knee,
Gently to disagree,
Gently to reinstruct,
To smite me in the heart
As deep as to the groin, to wake
Heartsease, heartbreak.
From that day forth I played the loving part.

And I saw this, and saw the ruin of lovers:
In the circle of parting, in the shadowline
Where dream meets doom, in the softly raining moment,
They come to half-lies, swerving without speaking.

1935

THE REFUGE IN THE FOREST

Today we have come
A long way from home:
From the prison camp
To the dark swamp,
From official words
To the scolding of birds,
From the rubber club
To the spider web,
From fiery skies
To the buzzing of flies.

Our fingers are cold
With the touch of the toad.
Our story is told
Near the snake's abode.
Our whispers cross
Through the hairy moss.
The well-housed snail
Studies our trail.
The blind moles hear
Our stumbling career.
The field-mouse squints
At our footprints.

How the human eye
Explodes in their sky!
Iris and white
Shine through the night.
The insects arm
And hum their alarm.
Small animals rush
Through the underbrush.
We laugh to see

How big we can be.
We are giant strangers
Among midget dangers.

Tomorrow we cross
The borders of loss
To walk a new land
As on quicksand,
To learn a tongue
Strange and singsong,
And words will waylay us
And laws will gainsay us.

Who are midget and strange
While the countries change,
Let's now fool away
This whole holiday:
For once giant strangers
Among midget dangers.

1939

THE OASIS

I thought I held a fruit cupped in my hand.
Its sweetness burst
And loosed its juice. After long traveling,
After so long a thirst,
       I asked myself: Is this a drought-born dream?
       It was no dream.

I thought I slipped into a hidden room
Out of harsh light.
In cushioned dark, among rich furnishings,
There I restored my sight.
       Such luxury could never be for me!
       It was for me.

I thought I touched a mind that fitted mine
As bodies fit,
Angle to curve; and my mind throbbed to feel
The pulsing of that wit.
       This comes too late, I said. It can't be true!
       But it was true.

I thought the desert ended, and I felt
The fountains leap.
Then gratitude could answer gratitude
Till sleep entwined with sleep.
       Despair once cried: No passion's left inside!
       It lied. It lied.

1987

CHANGES OF CLIMATE

Once I lived in polar night,
Burned summer fat for winter light.

When my store was nearly gone,
There came someone like Tropic sun.

I shed my clothes in so much heat
And the ice-mountains in retreat

Fled downhill over river-banks,
Sweat streaming from their white-skinned flanks.

Now, though all around I see
A fragrant moist community

Of fevered growth and sudden storm
Where insect generations swarm

And flesh is eager to divide
And fruit is roundly multiplied,

I dare not lose my Arctic skill,
My strategies against the chill:

What if the fire quit that face?
What if that sun shifted its place?

What if my clouds obscured its light?
What if I woke to daylong night?

Cold would then constrict this scene
And pinch the bud and bleach the green

And scatter those bright birds, all lost
In one shotgun blast of frost.

The giant tendrils withering,
Flesh shrinking into shivering,

Lichens and one stunted tree
Replacing this dense canopy,

And then, upon their well-worn track,
The ice-monsters lumbering back.

1982

GRAY HAIRS

Gray hairs
crowd out the black.
Not one of them
brings me wisdom.

Wrinkles
provide no armor.
I still quiver
to anyone's dart.

1980

WAKING IN ALARM
BEFORE THE ALARM

I try to return to the underwater canyons.
I try to drown, but the day pulls me back from drowning
By the hairs of my head, and every hair is fastened
To a painful thought.

Here, in the quick-changed scenes of the waning night,
Failure climbs over failure as if triumphant.
In a cold blue light, age bares its gums, and sickness
Mixes its poisons.

I try to return to the underwater canyons
And the salt creatures and their blind entwining,
But I drift above. My eyes remain wide open
Beneath closed lids.

I drift above. Till at last I am wholly awake
And streaming with light I stand on the shore of the day.
Now my dawn-phantoms
Withdraw, sun-dazzled.

1972

THE NIGHTMARE CAR

You're going downhill
towards the heart of town.
Your foot hits the floor:
the brakes are gone.

The steering wheel spins,
comes off in your hand.
Caught in your lights
the strangers stand.

Packed in the road
they stand and scream.
You shout, "I can stop!
It's only a dream!"

Then you dream that you wake
to explain, to deny
the dents in your fenders.
Traffic roars by.

1976

DELTA OF AGE

The more I pick up, the more I let go.
The wider my banks, the more sluggish I flow.
With silt from the mountains and the city's debris,
The slower the river, the nearer the sea.

1980

THE WEATHERVANE

If I stay
lying broadside to the wind,
to the one prevailing wind,
do not call it strength of mind:
it is just that I obey
pressure from another wind,
one your chimney smoke denies,
and the drifting of your skies.

1953

AGE: TWO VOICES

1.

My brain unused,
my hands unfilled,
my words unheard
in the day's loudness.

I joke in public
and mourn in private
the slack of the skin,
the ache of the bone.

And mourn the friends
I've lost to death
and friends alive
but lost to me.

This is the way
age goes about it:
first it robs you,
then it kills.

2.

What blasphemy
to rail at age
when only luck
got you this far!

Sickness, raiding
the streets of childhood,
seized your brother
but let you pass.

By luck, by luck,
by the width of an ocean,
you were not gassed
in the screaming chamber.

Not gouged by famine,
not scarred by war,
your body still
plays out its beat.

3.
My body still
plays out its beat
and praises age,
this patient friend,

and fights with age,
this robber who
ransacks my house
before it kills.

1990

IN THE HOSPITAL

She sits in her strong middle age
Near his white and iron cage

And strokes his arm, and feels thin bone
Beneath frail skin, and hears his moan,

That deep-voiced moan, that wavering call,
And cannot help. When he was small,

O redfaced cry that she could still!
O groping mouth that she could fill!

Now all her fiercely focused love
Cannot make his fingers move

And weakness holds him where there is
No exchange of hostages.

1983

FOUR EPITAPHS

1. DEATH OF THE FUGITIVE

No cash, no passport, papers not in order,
I crossed by chance this one unguarded border.
Police, stop short. Soldiers, stand at ease.
If you touch me now your hands will freeze.
Clerks and computers, when my name goes past
Close my dossier. This entry is the last.

1972

2. THE INVENTOR

I tried for a lifetime to design
an anti-noise machine,
a device to produce silence waves
of such wide nullitude
and high infrequency
that they could pass through walls
and bone
and membrane
and clear a path
through the cluttered brain
for the true messages.

My machine still unfinished,
Death fell upon me
and extinguished the noise,
but with it, all signals.

1977

3. THE MECHANIC

I was the healer and I could save
A powerful thing from a junkyard grave,
From the piled-up grave in the rusting sky.
O you who at full speed pass me by,
Do not turn to look: my lights are gone.
Darkness and I have crashed head-on.

1976

4. THE CHOICE

I wished to live
Neither as mirror nor as negative.
The lines were drawn, and I chose neither side.
Caught in that crossfire, I lived and died.

1993

RECOGNITION

Death the darkener
was also an illuminator,
and decorated your words
with gold-leaf.

With one gesture,
the same gesture
that silenced you,
Death attuned the ears of the young
to the ring of your voice.

And those failures
that in life
weighed like gravestones upon you
have become as light
as dried-out leaves.
They crumble, crumble.

1985

A DREAM OF PRISON

A caravan of bedbugs bears away
My blood by night, my memory by day.

From burns and beatings, memory is gone.
There was—I think there was—the raid at dawn,

The unmarked car. But what took place before
My stumbling answer to the shattered door?

Was it an act of mine that brought me here
Or random raiding by the torturer?

An act? What was my cause? Had I a cause?
These swollen hands made fists against whose laws?

Speak, my mute jailors! Somewhere, music blasts,
While in my fogbound mind, where nothing lasts,

I pound upon the stone of memory,
Tomb of my past.
                    What can he force from me,

The pale inquisitor with ice-blue eyes?
Robbed of my truth, how can I make up lies?

1993

FIRE IN THE CITY

The stoop is still there.
It leads nowhere.

The house burned down,
the beds burned black.

We came out alive
with roach and rat

and stand in the snow
and dare not look back.

We'll turn into salt
if we turn to look back.

1972

AN INHERITANCE

"Five dollars, four dollars, three dollars, two,
One, and none, and what do we do?"

This is the worry that never got said
But ran so often in my mother's head

And showed so plain in my father's frown
That to us kids it drifted down.

It drifted down like soot, like snow,
In the dream-tossed Bronx, in the long ago.

I shook it off with a shake of the head.
I bounced my ball, I ate warm bread,

I skated down the steepest hill.
But I must have listened, against my will:

When the wind blows wrong, I can hear it today.
Then my mother's worry stops all play

And, as if in its rightful place,
My father's frown divides my face.

1973

FACTORY POEM

The tool-bit cut, the metal curled,
The oil soaked through her clothing.
She made six hundred parts a day
And timed herself by breathing.

And what she made and where it went
She did not ask or wonder:
Gone to rust, or to machines
Of pleasure or of murder.

She dared not quit; she had seen those
Who fought like jackals over
The carcass of a rotting job
In cold Depression weather.

As if each payday would repay,
As if she'd live forever,
She wished away the newborn week
And wished the daylight over:

Evening bell, you I long for
With such restless longing
Come, straighten my shoulders
And deliver my hands.

1953

ON THE STREET

Her cough won't stop. Her bruises will not heal.
She plans her battle-plans for the next meal.
And she is mocked by smells from restaurants
And wasted warmth that steams from subway vents.
No place to hide between concrete and sky:
Snow or knife or eye of passerby
At any time can penetrate her rags.
Mumbling, she guards from thieves her plastic bags
And spreads her cardboard mattress for the night
In shallow doorways raw with sulphurous light.

Here is the pain outside of hospitals.
Here is the scribbled stench on city walls,
On walls of this high-towered metropolis
Whose sidewalks bear the mark of the abyss.
In this loud town, where easy money flows
All ways but down,
                    she walks in dirt-stiff clothes.

(New York City, Winter 1988)

IN THE BROKEN CITY

The small ghost
stood on the roof
and cried.

In the broken places
mother was searching
father was searching
both were crying
ghost was crying

in that thin voice
from the last roof.

1991

NIGHT PRAYER FOR
VARIOUS TRADES

Machinist in the pillow's grip,
Be clumsy and be blind
And let the gears spin free, and turn
No metal in your mind.

Long, long may the actress lie
In slumber like a stone,
The helpless words that rise from sleep
Be no words but her own.

Laborer, drift through a dark
Remote from clay and lime.
O do not tunnel through the night
In unpaid overtime.

You out-of-work, walk into sleep.
It will not ask to see
Your proof of skill or strength or youth
And shows its movies free.

And may the streetcleaner float down
A spotless avenue.
Who red-eyed wake at morning break
All have enough to do.

Enough to do. Now let the day
Its own accountings keep.
But may our dreams keep other time
Throughout our sprawling sleep.

1957

[87]

IN ANOTHER PART OF THE CITY:

A Vision out of Television

His burned-out childhood smoldered in the street.
Ankle-deep
In broken glass, he spoke as witness for
Each freezing kitchen and each gutted store.

Some watched him from far off, but watched in fear.
They lived in safety, but he loomed too near.
One feather-touch could make him disappear
If his rage came too near.

A few young ones among them, those who heard
Their secret phrases coded in each word,
Copied his every gesture enviously
And studied him as if he held their key.
He spoke so freely that they thought him free.

1993

AMONG THE GENTILES

As I walked in the land of the Gentiles,
As I walked in the land of my birth,
Curses lay buried like landmines
In that rich, that wheat-yielding earth.

So I watched my step with the Gentiles
And scanned every blue-eyed face.
My arms spread wide to keep balance
And sometimes spread wide to embrace.

The white skin I was wearing—
It served me, it kept me warm.
But the dark-skinned saw me wearing
A jailor's uniform.
My skin, so thin, so raggèd,
A jailor's uniform!

I'd laugh, if not for crying,
To walk in the world and see
The false clues strewn all over,
The barbed wire strung like tinsel,
The signs on the prisons juggled
With murderous irony.

1970

MEMORY OF A PARTY

You were young; you made a fool of yourself.
Oho, how you made a fool of yourself!
In front of the clever people,
in front of the clever people.

And they loosed upon you
the speared battalions of their wit.
You fell
into the dust of shame.
You were dragged by the heels
around the gates of their city.

Since that time
the clever ones
have, one by one,
been disarmed
of their toy weapons.
The city
has slowly
turned into a village.

That mock battle
took place long ago
among all the real wars.
But its memory has the power
to hammer in your head,
make the sweat start,

as though your own stupidity
could explain all loss.

Still, today you would be willing
to go through that evening again,
even in slow motion,

just to feel once again
the smooth taut skin
of your young face
speaking its foolishness.

1972

HARE AND TORTOISE

August, that crawled
in its carapace of sweat,
ran by too swiftly.

1987

A VISIT TO MATHLAND

(for M., Z., and L., citizens thereof)

I was a timid tourist
to the land of mathematics:
how do you behave in a country
where Reason rules?

Under that stern government
I found a land of play.

The roller-coasters of their curves!
The infinite tricks to be played
with all the infinities
plus one!
How elegant
were the formal gardens
of their proofs!
There, even chaos
had its own designs!

Every number I met
in the great cities of the Numbers
had its unique visage among the crowd,
its hooded mystery, its magic,
its own sure place
in a clean and ordered world.

It was a brief trip.
The altitude frightened me.
The pure air made me dizzy.
I fumbled in the language
(though I did like the natives).

And I was homesick for my homeland,
the Swamp of Ambiguity
that breeds its own fevers.

1962

AFTER THE ARGUMENT

Scraping a burnt pot,
she broods on a botched life,

then scrubs the floor
to placate the Furies.

The pot shines.
The floor shines.

1974

IN THE WOODS

They walked in the world together
And came to the end of play.
Each of them clung to the other
And each pushed the other away.

That forest was not so scary,
And two should be warmer than one.
But each was so scared for the other
They shivered in spite of the sun.

And each so resembled the other,
Fear saw only its twin.
Neither could harbor the other,
Though skin touched answering skin.

Then they stood and swore at each other
To stop that trembling inside,
Till a chill came forth from their bodies
And the leaves that touched them died.

The birds flew off with the crumbs,
Thunderclouds rolled overhead,
And at last they fled from each other,
In grief and relief they fled.

1967

LOSS IN LOS ANGELES

Outside, unmoving smog.
How can there be a hurricane in your head?
Around you, gardens too sweetly scented.
How can you contain wilderness?
The rainy season is over.
What is that wet on your cheeks?

1962

THE FALL

All that power
suddenly departing,
casting her down
to a desolate place.

It cast her down
from so high up,
she almost landed
below the ground.

A sleeping dog she is,
a drowning log she is,
a crumpled rag she is,
tired, so tired.

Slowly she comes back
sullenly she comes back
to her own body.
It takes her in.

It takes her in,
enfolds her motherly,
and never questions
where she has been.

1972

JEALOUSY

From five hundred miles away
jealousy can hear
the crumpling of a pillow
beneath two heads.

1961

THE DANGEROUS WORLD

I watched you walk across the street,
Slightly stooped, not seeing me,
And smiled to see that mixture of
Clumsiness, grace, intensity.

Then suddenly I feared the cars,
The streets you cross, the days you pass.
You hold me as a glass holds water.
You can be shattered like a glass.

1981

THE THINGS

The things that had blessed them
began to conspire against them.
The food burned
the glass broke
the bed narrowed
the words withered.

1968

PRESENTS FOR IAN

A purple thistle
that has no sting,
a fossil snail
that's still crawling.

An upside-down
drop of rain,
a talking fish,
a frog soprano.

A wave in a cave
the size of your thumb,
an agate marble
as big as the sun.

Keep them in
a treasure box
made of live oak trees
with a blue-sky lid.

And live oaks twisting
and blue sky shining
and yellow hills uncurling
as you rush forward.

1983

THE CONTRARY MUSE

Poet *(kneels stiffly)*:

I beg you, Muse, come down, come down and redeem me!
You used to arrive any time, you would come for no reason.
Now, though the sweat of death stood on my forehead,
No song would be shaken.

Muse:

I pay no heed to prayers or to reproaches.
I bless those who burn, but they must not burn only for me.
Turn your passion elsewhere. Then, when least you remember
My touch, I may touch you.

1983

TRYING TO PAINT CLOUDS

Trying to paint clouds,
I fix my feet to the ground.

O white travelers
with your umber bellies
rushing through
that blue neighborhood!
So much speed up above,
I spin backwards down below.
So much change up above,
my brush is outraced
every swirling second.

1986

BLANK PAGE

When I have fears that I may cease to be
Before my pen has gleaned my teeming brain...
                                           —John Keats

My fear is this: that I may keep on being
when my brain no longer teems.
What then,
poor gleaner,
stooping
in the miserly fields?

1990

CLARITY

The bone-white white pebbles in the brook,
a red leaf caught among them.

1960

OSCAR WILDE IN READING GAOL

I know not whether Laws be right
Or whether Laws be wrong.
All that we know who lie in gaol
Is that the wall is strong,
And every day is like a year,
A year whose days are long.

—Oscar Wilde,
"The Ballad of Reading Gaol"

The Law was wrong but it was strong,
And fragile was his case.
No words of wit could strengthen it
Or soften the judge's face
Or save outrageous Oscar Wilde
From outrage and disgrace.

Who could forgive that he could live
In bedroom and salon
Not by the Rules of Queensberry
But with Queensberry's son?
And so with all due process they
Locked him in steel and stone.

Yes, punishment it punishes
And maybe it deters.
Hard labor sears the flesh, they said,
Till Lust no longer stirs.
So let this aesthete pose among
Forgers and murderers.

With aching ear and pasty skin
He served the full two years,
Glimpsed Madness from his three-plank bed,

Most fierce of all his fears.
His aphoristic elegance
Was drained in pus and tears.

And Cleverness, like friends, withdrew,
And then Despair gave tongue.
The Law was wrong, the wall was strong,
But Pity walked among
The silent men on prison-rounds
And shaped that mournful song.

1990

DISCOVERY

I followed a thought all day
But I followed as if to slay.
My face had a hunter's cast.
All thought went bounding past.

Drowsing and careless I lay.
A wild thought came my way.
It saw me while I was blind.
It sprang to my slumbering mind.

1955

INSCRIPTION FOR
A SMALL PAINTING

Straw-yellow hills
Merge in green crotches.
In the dawn-valleys
Plumes of Pacific fog.

1983

SHE ADDRESSES THE WIFE

Do not stand and tremble
When you think of me.
Your castle may be sand
But I am not the sea.

Nor am I a refuge
Nor am I a throne.
I am the dark streets
A man walks alone.

Alone, alone he walks
And he sings at will
And at will departs
And my streets are still.

Though at moments I
Heard his helpless cry
It was not you he yielded
In that yielding sigh.

We came out into twilight
Separate and free.
Each encounter died
Of its own secrecy.

Now, though your rage
Could turn me to stone,
Let your eyes just once
Fasten on my own.

1952

FRAGMENT OF A NIGHT

That curved carved mouth,
that tender much-inventing wandering mouth!
I could say more. But now my lips are sealed.

1985

THE WEEPING SEA-BEAST

Tentacled for food,
You range your underwater neighborhood.

To look, to like, to eat, to break your fast!
Before you move an inch an hour is past,

Your prey is past, a swarm of scales, an eye,
A round fish eye, a rude unblinking eye.

You close on nothing; slowly you untwine
Your many arms and trail them through the brine.

Now sailors at the surface hear you cry,
And from those heights they cannot fathom why.

For there are agile creatures all around
Who dart like flames through this rich hunting ground,

And others who lie still and gaping wide
And make no move; but armies come inside.

1965

I MET MY SOLITUDE

I met my Solitude. We two stood glaring.
I had to tremble, meeting her face to face.
Then she saying, and I with bent head hearing:
"You sent me forth to exile and disgrace,

"Most faithful of your friends, then most forsaken,
Forgotten in breast, in bath, in books, in bed.
To someone else you gave the gifts I gave you,
And you embraced another in my stead.

"Though we meet now, it is not of your choosing.
I am not fooled. And I do not forgive.
I am less kind, but did you treat me kindly?
In armored peace from now on let us live."

So did my poor hurt Solitude accuse me.
Little was left of good between us two.
And I drew back: "How can we stay together,
You jealous of me, and I laid waste by you?

"By you, who used to be my good provider,
My secret nourisher, and mine alone.
The strength you taught me I must use against you,
And now with all my strength I wish you gone."

Then she, my enemy, and still my angel,
Said in that harsh voice that once was sweet:
"I will come back, and every time less handsome,
And I will look like Death when last we meet."

1959

PART III

NEW AND UNCOLLECTED POEMS

TO COVER WITH SEAWEED HIS IMAGE

To cover with seaweed his image,
to banish his tallness
into the caverns of the mind!
His profile was like a bird.
Fly away! Fly away!

Somewhere in the world
his long legs and arms.
Play, be charming to others,
suffer the world's demands,
but whistle to me no more,
to my remembering be ogre!

If only it were an ogre
who swallowed that part of my youth
then might my tears hold blame,
my soft curses follow someone.

To cover with seaweed his image!

1936

THE SAILOR LANDBOUND

Leafgreen of green
Fastened to the ground.
It will not shift or swell
Or sink and be drowned.

Upright is the window,
Steady the door,
Solid the citizens
On the unmoving floor.

No wind tears at a cry
To embrace and erase.
Here, sound is a juggler
Juggling my face.

Here, what is offered
Is to leave or to take.
What I leave will not
Vanish in my wake.

The door is to answer,
The debt is to pay.
Tomorrow will not find me
Miles from yesterday.

1946

MODERN SORCERY

One shining drop of hate distilled
Can go diffusing endlessly
To poison you and poison me
And all the fish in all the sea.

1950s

CLAY

I was clay
Your thumb print gave me
Even your idleness
humble and willing

Here I am,
my yielding form

and answered quickly.
a restless thought.
wrought me readily,
to work of hands.

harder than you,
fixed by fire.

1950s

REVELATIONS

Saints were revealed as murderers.
Paradise
had gangrened fingers
in its ice suburbs.
Confessions
so richly detailed
were forced, were false.

We had swallowed
truth and lies
ground together in a paste.
Now our shame
is a hooded cobra
in a house without windows or doors
in a corner we dare not approach.

1950s

THE FACTORY GIRL'S FAREWELL

Morning bell, from now on
I am deaf to your summons.
Evening bell, you I prayed for,
Urging the clock-hand,
You move me no longer.
Not for me your release.

Shopmates, I leave you
My pliers, my hammer,
My lunch box, my work-smock
And all my bad jokes.

If anyone asks you
What I am doing
Say I'm in the kitchen
Say I'm in the kitchen.

Here soap and water
Will wrinkle my fingers
Far from the grime now
Far from the grease.

Eyes of potatoes
See how I've changed now
Heart of the onion
Hush don't you cry...

1951

THE THINGS, THE ANIMALS

for Jules Supervielle

Today was a loud day,
a day that stunned the ear.
But taking up your book
I know I still can hear.
For I can harbor these
soft-spoken visitors,
the things, the animals
that are at home in you
as in a fairy tale.
That heart so hesitant
but chief among the guests.
The riddles of that bird,
the answers of that lamp.
The not-so-silent fish
who bring word of the drowned.
The street whose every stone
cries Paris to the world.

They come, they bring their friends.
and each is eloquent.
Their voices enter me
through any door they find.
Now this loud day withdraws
to its allotted place
among the other days
and there it is become
a thing, an animal
that looks from liquid eyes,
speaks softly, if at all.

1953

INTO SKID ROW

Pitiless the posters blaze on him,
The faces of success burn down on him,
The palm trees stiffly turn their backs on him.
He tells his failures like a rosary.

Look up, look up, see in the shimmering sky
What hovers there and waits for him to fall.
If once he falls, if to one knee he falls,
How soon will pawnshops pick him clean and bare.

And clean and bare what will be left of him?
He stumbles through the waste that wasted him.
The fount of alcohol runs dry for him.
The throat goes dry that even speaks of him.

(Los Angeles, 1956)

SCHOOL INTEGRATION SCENE, 1957

The children come
to the white fortress.
Silently they walk
through spit and curses
from angry grown-up faces:
pale distorted visages
that show the ravages
of a disease
endemic for centuries.

SONG OF THE OUTERMOST CASTE

Motherland, are you my mother?
Motherland, I have no other.
Though you wear a smiling mask,
You've set me a nightmare task:

Bade me build but banned my home,
Closed my school and called me fool.
Used my strength, then feared my strength.
Hired me last and fired me first.

And your talk is double-talk
And your word belies your deed
And your deed has scarred my back,
Motherland, my motherland...

Yet even when I speak my wrong
I speak it in my mother tongue.

about 1960

WHITE FOG BLUES

(for voice and harmonica)

White fog all around you,
         fog creeps into your clothes.
Fog so thick around you,
         wear it just like clothes.
Can't see the cars come creeping,
         don't know where this street goes.

Listen to that ship moaning,
         moaning like it's blind.
That ship, that foghorn moaning,
         moaning like it's blind.
Hold tight, if once you lose me,
         No one else will you find.

Street may be full of people,
         feels like you're all alone.
Street full of stumbling people,
         feels like you're all alone.
Hug the wall if you find it,
         caught so far from home.

White fog round your shoulders,
         wrapped around your mind.
It holds you round the shoulders,
         it's heavy on your mind.
Go groping up the alleys,
         every alley is blind.

1960s

RUNNING OUT OF CITIES

From the concrete city of my birth
I ran to discover some earth.
In the city of the palm
I found no calm.
In the City of Light
I made my own night.
In the city of fog
I was stuck in a bog.
Out of cities I ran
Back to where I began
Till I spent all the wealth
Of the city of Self.

1964

THE RIVER-LOVER

Turn away from the window
And tell me what you see.
Myself in the deep dark river
And no raft under me,
No raft under me.

But I will be your river.
I twist I turn I flow.
Lapped in dark motions you will lie
Who lie in me below.

And afterwards, and afterwards?
For still the dawn comes on.
The sun will shatter the window,
The water-sucking sun.

I'll be your peaceful river.
One breath will make me shiver,
One leaf will make me quiver,
In the warm-bodied dawn.

about 1967

DEATH AND THE EXILE

— Who's that climbing up the stairs?
Who's that knocking at my door?
Who's that sitting in my chair?
   Said the bone-tired exile.

— It's only me, who else could it be,
With rain on my head from another countree.
Now put down your pen and come with me.
   Said the skull-faced stranger.

— I have no passport, how can I go,
And no identity card to show,
And my bribe-money was spent long ago.
   Said the bone-tired exile.

—You need no papers to go with me.
I cut through red tape as easily
As you can cut through an artery.
   Said the skull-faced stranger.

about 1965

KORCZAK AND THE ORPHANS

He made his choice.
He went with them.
Their eyes so large,
their ribs so plain.

They walked, a thin
and straggling line,
past beefy,
booted,
grinning guards.

In the bookkeeping
of the butchers
how small an entry
this would make:
192 children,
13 adults.

1970

DREAMING

A DRAMA IN HUNDREDS OF THOUSANDS OF ACTS

In your closed and curtained mind
You watch a play when you are blind.
The cast flies in from everywhere
To tread a stage that is not there.
A brilliant cast! They learn each part
Instantaneously by heart.
No critics come to cramp their style,
Praise their inventions, or revile
Their posturing, their speech deranged,
The scenery in mid-sentence changed.

But every scene makes sense to you.
Director: you, and Author: you.
You find the costumes and the props
In your life's attic, not in shops.
You build the sets, design the lights,
Stage-manage this and all the nights,
You lead the cast, you are the cast,
You come on first, you come on last,
You come to say the play is done.
Goodbye, you audience of one.

1970s

OBSERVATIONS

Epitaph: The Clown

I thought up jokes to be my epitaph
But could not make His Royal Grimness laugh.

*

New York Summer

Summer streets crackling
with human lightning.

*

Traffic

So much traffic
in the passageway to death
you'd think it would slow things down.

*

The Muse Offended

If you force the Muse,
she turns into Medusa.

*

You Watch Your Words

You watch your words.
In that glaring light
all color is blanched from them.
Be wasteful!
Does autumn
embalm each leaf?

*

Living on Little...

Living on little in a world of lack
Easily she breathed the common air.
Living on little in a world of glut
She gasped for air in envy and despair.

*

Armor

Undress yourself of that armor
made useless by new weapons.

*

Vision

In the moist caverns
by the sound of her breathing
he finds his way in the dark.

*

Styles

Summer sorrow
wears different clothing
from winter sorrow.

*

Age 15

On a winter street
the huddled warmth of friends
hunched up with laughter.

*

Worrier

Even the trivial
came cloaked in terror.
And then she faced
the truly terrible.

*

(These short poems written at various times: 1960–2000)

A LITERARY NOTE

Once upon a time
in a country without a written language
a woman sang a song to her child.
In its grandeur
and melancholy
and simplicity
it surpassed all poems ever in books,
even in the nine lost books of Sappho.

Though this cannot be proven,
I swear it happened.

1970s

COWARD COME TO JUDGMENT

Take warning you fearful,
take warning from me
or you'll wake up some morning
and see what I see.

Your palms will ache
your poor hands will shake
with all the caresses
you dared not make.

What is that red
in the bloodshot eye?
The dammed-up tears
you dared not cry.

If you had friends
fear made you disown,
they'll stand, arms linked,
where you stand alone.

A crime you saw
when fear kept you mute
will stomp on your spine
with its torturer's boot.

While all the lies
you were scared to deny
are a stinging swarm
in a thunderhead sky.

This Valley of Dread
you'll have to pass through
when, empty of mercy,
you judge you.

about 1973

ESTRANGEMENT

I don't need them! I don't need them!
They didn't need me so I don't need them!

Yet their whispered names can reach me still
Above the roar of a pneumatic drill.

That room's an abyss where they might appear.
I laugh the louder if they might hear.

For here is the working of my contrary mind:
My loyal friends are of humankind;
They're fallible, mortal, they may be blind.

But those who spurn me: they must see
With the unblinking eyes of deity.

Did they look in my soul with their x-ray eyes?
What cowardice, envy, social lies,

What secret betrayals did they see?
What godlike judgment did they pass on me?

They turned away and never said why.
I thought I would die. I didn't die.

See, in the world I dance and sing:
I don't need them for anything.

But sometimes into my soul I creep
When I'm huddled up in the swamp of sleep.

As in an old movie I see them again.
And all is so easy and flowing again.

Then they turn away. I ask them: Why?
And once again there is no reply.

about 1976

AUTOMATIC WRITING

I instructed my hand to write of green hills,
or of the jeweled windows of skyscrapers
seen across the park
in winter twilight.

Instead it took off all on its own
to write of age, loss, death.

about 1985

DEATH OF AN ACTOR

(in memoriam, C.L.)

He could play any part in any voice.
He could loose thunderbolts of tragedy
Or shift one hip and curl his lip to farce.
Any mask was his but this death-mask.
What is it doing here on his young face?
This muteness unrehearsed, so stiff-composed—
This part's not his!

1987

THE HUMAN INTELLECT DIVINE

I love to see, in a naked face,
a generous intelligence displayed
in all its sensual grace.

about 1990

COLORS

Out of the fog
a spurt of vermilion.

     ...

Red pepper! A red
that would, in a dress,
be garish, vulgar.

     ...

A tent of vision
moving with us
along the fog-bound beach.

     ...

Pale surprised face
in the mirror:
an explosion of wrinkles.

     ...

Earth colors
and lamp black
in blue-ice caves.

     ...

From the city shore:
a yellow band of smog
between sea and sky.

     ...

Clouds, seeming
more solid than hills.

     ...

On the ice of the pond
under the bare weeping willow,
an empty green whiskey bottle.

     ...

The weight of snow on the shovel!
Those tiny white fragile crystals
added up to this!

     ...

Delicate ink tracks
across white paper
while black hair
goes grayer into night.

1990s–2002

GRIEVANCES PRESENTED TO THE BOSS, THE MUSE OF LYRIC POETRY, BY THE INTERNATIONAL UNION OF LYRIC POETS

1.   You never set us the job to do.
but we feel your sickening displeasure
if it is not done,
and done well.

2.   You don't pay by the hour
or by the week, or by the year.
One of us could labor a lifetime
and never earn your smile
yet look how you bless that other one
who turned out a piece
in one dizzying day.

3.   You have no precision instruments
to gauge the value of our finished products.
(Your inspectors keep changing
and some have little love for you.)

4.   You lock us into our language
even when our homeland is cold to us.
The more precise our words,
the more they dazzle in their music and play,
the harder it is for them
to cling to their beauty
when they try to cross a border.

5.   You promote the young among us.
What should the old workers do?
Learn a new trade?
You even expect these frail old ones
to compete with their young selves.
We demand a pension for Aesthetic Security
and a small dole of Wisdom
to get us through the winter.

6.   You let us keep up production
when there's no demand.
Our pieces clog the market.
No one stops to listen.
Must we blame our own shoddiness?

7.   We have grievances. We grieve.
But we won't ever go out on strike.
We fear your lockout
as we fear death.
Once you took us on for this job
we thought it was for life.

1995

CATALOGUE

1.

My blurring eyes, my deafened ears—
O careless sadism of the years!

Sun-loving and sun-ravaged skin—
One-sided love has done you in.

My teeth—less said, less missed! — my heart—
My runaway, my telltale heart—

Heart whose misfirings can defeat
The pulse of this iambic beat!

(While hypochondria detects
Whatever ill it hears of next.)

2.

In couplets that are not heroic
I try to say, in accents stoic:

For every rusting body-fetter
Perhaps my wit will work the better.

I will not be subservient
To every ruined ligament!

I'll prove on my anatomy
A body-mind dichotomy!

3.

Brave words! No use! I cannot force
Such an unnatural divorce.

My body! You have stood by me
Through insult and through injury

Some eighty years. How can my mind,
Seeing you slow, not lag behind?

Its sharpness dulls, yet feels each ache.
How not to mourn for your sweet sake?

My generous, my failing host,
O do not yet give up this ghost.

Kindle for me a little spark,
For I am whistling in the dark.

2002

WHERE IS URSULA?

Where is Ursula, I wonder.
By some billabong Down Under?

In rainforest Spanish-mossed?
Tiptoeing on permafrost?

Skiing down some slippery slope?
Rounding Capes of Stubborn Hope?

On an island coconut-palmed?
In Horse Latitudes becalmed?

Discovering a new Lascaux?
Studying Basque and Navajo?

I know exactly where I am—
Ninety-Fourth and Amsterdam—

Multi-planar, where is she?
What dimension, what degree?

Comes she hither? Goes she yonder?
Is she wearing a transponder?
Where is Ursula, I wonder.

2003

UNFINISHED

—Why are you hurrying?

—I have a deadline.
 I have a deathline.

 Before a stroke strikes me
 Or my heart skips out on me
 Or cancer crawls through me
 Or confusion addles me,

 I hurry, I hurry
 To chip away
 At the wall of my silence.

2007

ON A SPLINTERED BOARDWALK

In our decrepit seaside town,
Full of life but falling down,

The air is clean, rents are low,
Jobs are scarce and buses slow.

Where the hemmed-in, channeled sea
Laps the shoreline timidly,

Muscled youths advance and prance
In acrobatic arrogance.

Poets chant and rock-bands drum.
Wheelchairs turn to catch the sun.

Faded signs announce the past.
Sagging boardwalks will not last.

Steel and glass, cold as cash,
With one wrecking ball can smash

All the termite-riddled wood
Of our fragile neighborhood,
Its many-colored decrepitude.

1965, 2009

DEEP BLUE

Sky so bright and you so blue.
Sadness screams inside of you,
And that noise can drown all else
With its furious decibels.

When you laugh, that laugh is forced.
When you speak, each word's rehearsed.
Worrier, you guess the worst.
Days are danger, dreams are cursed.

Reason argues: This will pass—
Craziness! It cannot last!
Loss of sleep and death of hope
Will become an anecdote,

One that you will live to tell,
Unmedalled veteran of hell:
How the blues once wrapped you round
(Ashes! Ashes! All fall down!)

2009

WALKING BACK

Did I go there?
Did I say that?
Ashamed, I deny it.
Proud, I affirm it.

Those are my tracks.
So easy to lose them
in swamps, in lush grass,
in crowds, on concrete.

Old maps outworn,
new ones undrawn,
landmarks defaced
by storm or by vandals.

Initials carved
in ancient trees,
children shouting
in a changed grammar.

Was I that child
who looks back at me?
Her spine is straighter,
her gaze is clearer.

2010

ABOUT NOT WRITING

Tongue-tied, I stand before
Myself as inquisitor.

I loved to mark time
With a beat, with rhyme.

Time marked me with its thumb,
Slowed down the pendulum.

Slowed it down, or stopped:
Words were lopped, words dropped—

No use to devise
Reasons or alibis.

Now, strangely, I draw breath
Well past my ninetieth.

What's begun is almost done,
Still I must brood upon

The much that I sought,
The little that I wrought,

Till Time brings its own
Lockjaw of stone.

2011

PART IV
A FEW TRANSLATIONS

ON THE TRANSITORY

(from the German of Hugo von Hofmannsthal)

My cheeks still feel their breath: how can it be
That these most recent days, these days just past,
Are gone, forever gone, gone totally.

Here is a thing no one can wholly grasp,
Too terrible for tears or for complaint:
That all goes by, that all goes flowing past,

And that this Self of mine, all unconstrained,
Came gliding straight to me from a small child,
Came like a dog uncanny mute and strange,

And: that I was, a hundred years ago,
And my ancestors in their death-shrouds are
As close to me as my own hair is close,

As much a part of me as my own hair.

BALLADE OF OUTER LIFE

(from the German of Hugo von Hofmannsthal)

And children grow up and their eyes are deep.
They know of nothing; they grow up, they die,
And everybody follows his own path.

And fruits that first are sour grow into sweetness
Until at night they fall down like dead birds
And there for a few days they lie and rot.

And still and always blows the wind, and we
Can understand and utter many words
And sense the joy and tiredness of the limbs.

And streets run through the grass and here and there
Are places full of torches, trees, and ponds,
And all is threatening, and deathly withered...

Why then were they made? And each one never
Just like another? And why countless many?
And changing— laughing, weeping, growing pale?

What use is this to us, and all these games,
To us, grown-up and forever lonely,
And wandering, never seeking any goal?

What use, to have seen so many things like this?
And yet whoever says *evening* says so much—
Deep melancholy flowing from that word

Like heavy honey from the hollow comb.

THE BIRD

(from the French of Jules Supervielle)

—Bird, what are you looking for, fluttering over my books?
All in this small room is alien to you.

—I do not know your room, I am far away.
I never left my woods, I am on the tree
Where my nest is hidden: understand otherwise
Whatever is happening, forget a bird.

—But I see your beak, your feet, and see them close.

—Then you know how to bring the distance towards you.
If your eyes find me, that is not my fault.

—You must be here, because you answer me.

—I answer the fear I always have of men.
I feed my young and that is all I do.
I keep them hidden in the darkest part of a tree
That I thought thick and safe as one of your walls.
Hold back your words and leave me on my branch.
I fear your thoughts as I do a rifle shot.

—Then quiet the heart that hears me through the feathers!

—What horror hid in your dark gentleness!
Ah you have killed me I fall from my tree.

—I must be alone; even the look of a bird...

—But I tell you I was far, I was deep in my woods!

FACES

(from the French of Jules Supervielle)

Against my will, I take
The faces dear to me
And shuffle them like cards.
At times I let one fall.
I look for it in vain,
The card has disappeared.
I hear no more of it.
Still, it was a good face,
And I loved it well.
I mix the other cards.
The unrest of my room,
I mean by that my heart,
Is agitated still,
But not for the lost card.
Another takes its place,
Another, a new face.
And so the deck is full
But always mutilated.
That is all I know,
Nobody knows more.

ALONE

(from the Yiddish of Itzakh Manger)

No one here knows what I want.
No one listens when I speak.
Seven little mice and one more mouse
On the floor asleep.

Seven little mice and one more mouse—
That makes eight, you know.
I put my cap upon my head,
Say goodnight, and go.

I put my cap upon my head
And I'm off on my own.
Where should I go so late at night
All by myself alone?

A tavern in the square cries out,
Come on inside, you fool!
I've got a barrel full of wine,
A barrel full of gold.

I push the door, I rush inside,
Look around, and say,
"Everybody in the place,
Happy holiday!"

No one here knows what I want,
No one listens when I speak.
Two drunk men and a single flask
On the floor asleep.

Two drunk men and a single flask—
That adds up to three.
Play a fourth one in that game?
No, thanks, not for me!

I put my cap upon my head
And I'm off on my own.
Where should I go so late at night
All by myself alone?

I, LAÏS ...

(from the Greek of Plato)

I, Laïs, whose beauty was so great
That I could scorn all Greece, I, to whose door
Young lovers came in crowds, now dedicate
This mirror of mine to Aphrodite, for
What now I am I have no wish to see,
What once I was it will not show to me.

DREAM-POWERS

(from the German of Nikolaus Lenau)

The dream was so wild, the dream was so bad,
So deeply shaking and endlessly sad,
A dream so filled with ill:
I try to believe that I slept sound,
That I had no dream, that I slept sound,
But still I feel the tears run down,
And my heart hammers still.

I wake in weariness and fear.
Between the pillow and the wall
My handkerchief lies wet, as though
Some mourner at a funeral
Had used it so, and left it here.
Was it in dream I used it so,
Wiping my face? I do not know.

And yet I know that they were here.
The evil visitors appeared
And held their nightly revels here.
I slept; unguarded was my house.
The door stood wide, they came inside,
They came to feast and to carouse,
These wild intruders in my house,
And then departed from the place.
But in my tears I find their trace:
How they brought chaos to what was mine
And on the table spilled the wine.

WAR SONG

(from the German of Matthias Claudius)

War! It's war! Oh angel, speak against it!
    Protect us, in God's name!
Alas, it's war. And for this war
    I want to bear no blame.

What would I do if ghosts of all the fallen
    Came to me as I slept
And stood before me, stood there pale and bloody,
    And looked at me and wept?

And if brave men, the seekers after glory,
    Now in death agony
Rolled in the dust with shattered limbs before me
    And died there, cursing me?

And if the wives, the fathers and the mothers,
    So fortunate before,
All now made poor by war, laid waste by war,
    Came, clamored at my door?

If Plague and Hunger gathered in one grave
    Friend, friend and enemy,
And then alighted on a corpse, and crowed
    Their homage unto me?

How then could I rejoice in crown and honors,
    In gold and land and fame?
Alas, it's war. And for this war
    I want to bear no blame.

THE SWAMP

(from the German of Bertolt Brecht)

I saw many friends, and among them the friend I loved most,
Helplessly sink into the swamp
I pass by daily.
And a drowning was not over
In a single morning. Often it took
Weeks; this made it more terrible.
And the memory of our long talks together
About the swamp, that already
Had claimed so many.

Helpless now I watched him leaning back
Covered with leeches
In the shimmering
Softly moving slime:
Upon the sinking face
The ghastly
Blissful smile.

NOTES

On the dating of various poems throughout the book:
Since many poems were written over a period of years, dates are only approximate. The new and uncollected poems in Part III are arranged in roughly chronological order.

"The Refuge in the Forest" was written after the end of the war in Spain.

"Deep Blue." "Ashes, ashes, all fall down" is from the children's singing game, "Ring around the Rosie."

"Korczak and the Orphans." Janusz Korczak was a well-known Polish-Jewish educator and writer. Director of an orphanage for Jewish children under the Nazi occupation of Poland, he chose to stay with the children when they were evacuated to the killing camps, though he could have been saved by influential friends. Korczak, twelve staff members, and all the children were murdered.

Both Hofmannsthal poems are in a modified *terza rima* in the original.

The translation of "I, Laïs ..." is dedicated to the memory of Vera Lachmann, who after retirement gave free lessons in Ancient Greek in her Greenwich Village living room in the 1960s.

ACKNOWLEDGMENTS

Poems in the first part are from *Ring Song* (Scribner, 1952). Several poems appeared for the first time in the following publications: *Negro Quarterly*: "Whodunit" (under the title "Detective Story"); *Twice A Year*: "A Visit to the Zoo," "Restless Dialogue," "Ceremony" (under the title "The Man From Mars Goes Traveling"); *Art and Action*: "You Walked a Crooked Mile," "Take the Snake," "The End"; *Masses and Mainstream*: "The Money Tree," "The Six Million"; *California Quarterly*: "Housing Shortage."

Poems in the second part are from *The Dangerous World* (Another Chicago Press, 1994). Several poems appeared for the first time in the following publications: *Ploughshares*: "In the Hospital"; *Puckerbrush Review*: "After the Argument," "Factory Poem"; *Frank* (Paris): "The Inventor"; *Feminist Studies*: "Changes in Climate," "The Fall," "Waking in Alarm Before the Alarm"; *New York Quarterly* and *Geography of Poets* (Field, ed., Bantam): "An Inheritance"; *New York Quarterly*: "Fire in the City"; *Missouri Review*: "Death of the Fugitive"; *Against Infinity: An Anthology of Mathematical Poetry* (Robson and Wimp, eds., Primary Press): "A Visit to Mathland"; *Poetry in Public Places*: "Factory Poem"; *San Francisco Review*: "I Met My Solitude"; *Dacotah Territory*: "Jealousy," "Among the Gentiles"; *The Nation*: "The Weeping Sea-Beast"; *Poetry*: "She Addresses the Wife" (under the title, "The Mistress Addresses the Wife"); *Coastlines* (Los Angeles): "Night Prayer for Various Trades."

The third part is a selection of previously uncollected poems, some written or finished since 1994, others completed earlier. First publications are as follows: "Catalogue" appeared in *Forward*; "Death and the Exile" in *Bloom*. "Korczak and the Orphans" was first published in the anthology, *Blood to Remember* (2nd ed., Time Being Press, 2007).

Translations: The translation of Hugo von Hofmannsthal, "On the Transitory" was published in *World Poetry* (Norton, 1998). The translation of Matthias Claudius, "War Song," appeared in *Translation*, VI, Winter 1978–79. The translation of "Dream Powers" by Nikolaus Lenau appeared in *California Quarterly*. The translation of "The Swamp" by Bertolt Brecht was first published in *Poetry*, 1947.

My thanks to those who, in different ways, helped bring this book to light: Susan Barba, Jessica Breheny, Edward Field, Emily Grosholz, Patricia Grossman, Eric Gudas, Helene Kendler, X.J. Kennedy, Ursula K. Le Guin, Philip Levine, Joan Nestle, Estelle Gershgoren Novak, Marie Ponsot, Lynne Sharon Schwartz, Harvey Shapiro, Jean Valentine; and to the memory of Grace Paley, George Oppen, and Jane Cooper.

And to Eva Kollisch for her support in life and literature.

Author Photo by Robert Giard